SMALL QUILTS, BIG EVENTS

Julia LaBauve & Tammy Silvers

American Quilter's Society

P. O. Box 3290 • Paducah, KY 42002-3290

www.AmericanQuilter.com

Located in Paducah, Kentucky, the American Quilter's Society (AQS) is dedicated to promoting the accomplishments of today's quilters. Through its publications and events, AQS strives to honor today's quiltmakers and their work and to inspire future creativity and innovation in quiltmaking.

Executive Book Editor: Andi Milam Reynolds
Graphic Design: Barry Buchanan
Cover Design: Michael Buckingham
Photography: Charles R. Lynch

Additional copies of this book may be ordered from the American Quilter's Society, PO Box 3290, Paducah, KY 42002-3290, or online at www.AmericanQuilter.com.

Library of Congress Cataloging-in-Publication Data

LaBauve, Julia.
   Small quilts big events / by Julia LaBauve and Tammy Silvers.
      p. cm.
   ISBN 978-1-57432-650-5
   1. Patchwork--Patterns. 2. Quilting--Patterns. 3. Miniature quilts. I.
   Silvers, Tammy. II. Title.
   TT835.L235 2009
   746.46--dc22

                                    2009037716

CONTENTS

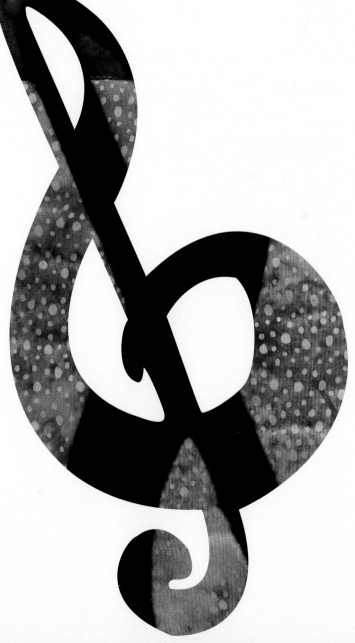

DEDICATION

To Steve Silvers and Joseph LaBauve, loving husbands who believe in us even when we don't

ACKNOWLEDGMENTS

We are indebted to many people who continually give us their love and support while we go out and dream of quilts to make:

Our husbands, Steve and Joseph, who always have opinions on our projects but who think all our quilts are beautiful;

Our faithful project testers—Ann D'Agostino, Melanie Gorby, and Molly Buwalda. These wonderful friends tested all our patterns carefully and had fun in the process;

Cassie Williams, who took our pictures and whose daughter, Brooke, provided the basis for the silhouette of the dancer in TUTU TERRIFIC; and

Andi Reynolds and the staff of AQS for believing thankfulness was something worth quilting about.

A heartfelt *Thanks!* to all who contributed to making this book a reality for us!

INTRODUCTION

Sometimes when we say "thanks" we feel that we are not saying enough, that we are not showing our appreciation in a manner that truly conveys how intensely grateful we are. This is how we, Julia and Tammy, felt not so long ago and what gave us the seed for this book.

We were already designing quilts together when, a few years ago, Julia's husband, Joe, received a pacemaker in order to keep his heart "ticking." It came as a surprise (Joe was in his late thirties at the time) and it was all done and over in three days. As Joe and Julia returned home from the hospital and reality sunk in, they realized how blessed they were that the pacemaker had saved Joe's life and that they had been in the hands of extremely competent nurses and doctors.

As their lives began to regain normalcy, Julia wanted to express her thanks to the nursing staff who had treated them with such care, compassion, and expertise. Still tired after the ordeal, Julia went into her sewing room ready to make a really cute "quilted something" for the staff. Well, she made a heart that looked like a kidney, and a project that looked more like a cartoon than a heartfelt "Thanks!"

How frustrating! She was not in the right frame of mind to just "come up" with something to make. What she needed was something already designed that she could make quickly and that conveyed what she felt. Sadly, the nurses never received that token of appreciation. Julia was not yet ready to create what she needed.

While all this was happening, Tammy gave Joe a quilted card with a bright red, crazy-quilted heart. The quilting even resembled EKG lines! Simple, and to the point.

This little quilted card was the beginning of *Small Quilts, Big Events*. Using a few red scraps and the "flip and stitch" method, Tammy created a patch of fabric large enough to cut the heart motif. The heart was then fused to the backing, stitched down with decorative machine stitching, and embellished with a tiny bit of machine embroidery mimicking the up/down of an EKG monitor to complete a heartfelt sentiment for Joe!

Photo enhanced

Joe loved his quilted card. That settled it! We knew we needed to create a set of patterns that other quilters could use whenever they needed something heartfelt, quickly. Not only for something as drastic as a pacemaker implantation, but to thank the vet who saved our beloved pet, the important teacher or coach in our child's life, or the friend standing by us in good and bad times—even just because we love someone and are thankful they are in our lives.

Use this book to say a big "Thanks!" with a small quilt to the people who truly make a difference in your life—those who are there with you for those big events of life. You can mix and match the motifs, the sayings, and the small 3" x 4" blocks. You can even make your own sayings from the complete alphabet included!

Go ahead, tell someone how extremely thankful you are for them and give them a small quilt that carries big thanks.

THE CONCEPT

So here you are: There is a person in your life to whom you want to show your heartfelt appreciation, but you do not have the time or energy it takes to make a quilt. Maybe you are not sure what to say. Don't worry! Our book is your solution!

SMALL QUILTS, BIG EVENTS quilts are designed so that on a simple quilted background, blocks, words, and motifs can be mixed and matched.

We've given you a series of small (that means doable in a short time) projects, all finishing 15" x 16", all easy to make out of just a few fat quarters, and all standardized. This "one size fits all" approach makes creating a special "Thank You" gift fast and easy but still thoughtful and very personal.

Templates and paper-piecing patterns begin on page 48.

All quilts follow the same layout:
- ♥ large border (A)
- ♥ small border (B)
- ♥ base (C)
- ♥ block column (D x 4)
- ♥ words
- ♥ motif
- ♥ binding (E)

Fig. 1

You can choose to make a project as shown in the book or interchange the blocks, words, and/or motif. And while there are many D blocks to choose from, they all finish to the same 3½" x 4½" dimensions.

Start by choosing from one of the 12 projects. The D blocks vary in each project, so if you prefer those for, say, YOU SHINE but are making LOVE MY VET, get the D block instructions from the YOU SHINE project.

Preparing and fusing the motifs; sewing pieces A, B, C, and the D column together; labeling; binding; and hanging your quilt are covered in Finishing Your Quilt on page 46.

Once you get a feel for how to make the D blocks and then incorporate them into the standard quilt layout, you are ready to go. This is an easy, relaxing project for you to do and a special gift for someone to receive. Show them how much you appreciate them and, in the process, have fun!

MATERIALS REQUIRED

These small quilts are all made using batik fat quarters and felted wool pieces. To make the quilt top you will need two different batiks that go well together. This creates a soft contrast when the blocks are pieced and sewn to the base and borders. The real "punch" comes in when the wool is fused to the quilt top. Choose pieces of wool that create a sharp contrast with the background and with each other.

All of our projects are completed using "repurposed" wool, as in wool that used to be an old coat, a skirt, or a worn pair of pants, and now have become a heart, house, or cross motif. We dyed and felted the fabric using bright, strong colors.

Wool, what a perfect match for batiks! In some of the projects we also mixed and matched solid wool with pieces that did not read as solids. When you are purchasing the wool, or if you are using some of the repurposed pieces, consider using checks, plaids, and similar designs. These elements add texture and interest to the project.

In the book, we refer to the batiks as light and dark fabrics. This is only a matter of naming convention. Usually, the dark fabric is used for pieces A, B, and parts of the D blocks, and the light one for C and parts of the D blocks.

More than the value of the fabrics, we used the scale of the motif as a placement guide. We placed the busiest fabrics alongside the edges of the quilt, that is A and B, while the fabric that read mostly as a solid was used as C. This helps the woolen motif to stand out even more, without competing with the design of the batik.

Because these are all small wallhangings, it is not necessary to prewash any of the fabrics. In fact, if you are using prewashed fabric, make sure you have enough for your project. Our fabric yardage recommendations are based on unwashed material. Just iron your fabric well and you will be ready to start!

When it comes to fusing wool, we tried several products readily available in the market. The best results were achieved using Wonder-Under® fusible web. This was the only product that yielded an evenly and strongly fused woolen motif to the cotton quilt top.

And speaking of fusing, we also used fusible batting. Because these are small projects, fusing the sandwich made it super easy to manipulate and sped up the whole process. Our projects are quilted using Hobbs Heirloom Fusible cotton batting.

Small Quilts, Big Events quilts are made using the typical tools of the trade— rotary cutters, rulers, mats, scissors, a sewing machine in good working order, and an iron/ironing board. Optionally (but this surely made our work easier), you can use a non-stick sheet for fusing the motifs to each other (and not to your ironing board!). We used the Appliqué Pressing Sheet from Bear Designs with excellent results.

CUTTING

Since pieces A, B, C, and E (binding strips) are the same dimensions for all projects, we recommend that you cut the fat quarters according to figures 2 and 3. You will have plenty left over to cut the strips and pieces for the D blocks. For consistency, all strips are cut 18" long, although sometimes this will yield leftovers.

Fig. 2

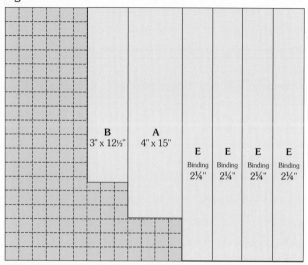

Fig. 3

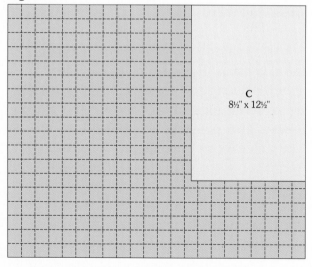

Make sure that your rotary-cutting tools are sharp and ready to cut. One big exception: do not use your "good" scissors to cut your wool. Using them will only make your good pair of scissors very dull, very quickly.

PRESSING

Pressing is very important during the construction of the blocks and the quilt top. Whenever possible, press to the dark. That is, press the seam towards the darker side so that you do not see any dark fabric underneath the lighter one when viewed from the front.

Also, as you sew the D blocks, be aware of how you press the seams. The blocks will lay much nicer if pieces are sewn so that the seams oppose each other as shown in figure 4.

Fig. 4

Verify that the final measurements are 3½" x 4½". If the block does not measure 3½" x 4½", go back to the ironing board and press the block again, making sure the fabric and all the seams are completely flat.

Sometimes, fixing ironing problems can give you the extra ⅛" needed to bring the block into the correct (or close to correct) dimensions.

If the block still does not meet the necessary measurements, you may have to choose between less than perfect points, an unsquare quilt, or making another block.

SPECIAL THANKS

Spiritual support is so important in our lives. From a minister to a friend, someone was there when you needed "just that something special." Thank them for their special presence in your life.

FABRIC AND MATERIALS

- ♥ Light batik - 1 fat quarter
- ♥ Dark batik - 2 fat quarters
- ♥ Backing - 1 fat quarter
- ♥ Felted wool:
    - Cross - 10" x 13" cream
    - Cross - 9" x 12" purple
    - Letters - 10" x 16" orange
    - Heart - 2" x 2" red
- ♥ Fusible web - 1 yard
- ♥ Fusible batting - one 19" x 20" piece
- ♥ Two plastic rings size ½"
- ♥ Templates (page 48)
    - Large cross
    - Small cross
    - Small heart (page 56)
    - Alphabet (pages 61 – 62)

CUTTING DIRECTIONS

* Set pieces A, B, C, and E aside while you make the D blocks. Once you have assembled the four 3½" x 4½" D blocks, you will sew the quilt top together.

LIGHT BATIK

One 1½" x 18" strip
Two 1¼" x 18" strips
One 8½" x 12½" rectangle (C)*

DARK BATIK

One 1½" x 18" strip
Two 1¼" x 18" strips
One 4" x 15" rectangle (A)*
One 3" x 12½" rectangle (B)*
Four 2¼" x 18" strips (E)*

MAKING THE D BLOCKS

Make one 2½" x 18" strip-set by sewing the light and dark 1½" x 18" strips right sides together. Press strips to the dark fabric.

Cut the 2½" x 18" strip-set into eight 2" x 2½" rectangles (fig. 1). Label these as rectangle 1.

Make two 2" x 18" strip-sets by sewing together a light and a dark 1¼" x 18" strip (fig. 2). Press strips to the dark fabric.

Cut these 2 strip-sets into eight 2½" x 2" rectangles. Label these as rectangle 2.

Following figure 3, lay out and sew 4 blocks that look like figure 4. Press.

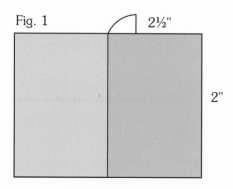

Fig. 1

2½"

2"

Rectangle 1

Fig. 2

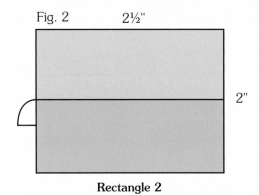

2½"

2"

Rectangle 2

Fig. 3

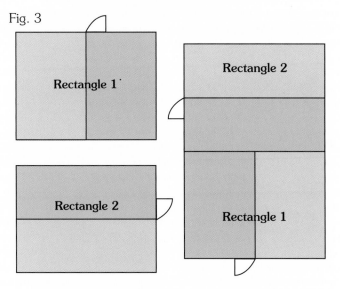

Rectangle 1

Rectangle 2

Rectangle 2

Rectangle 1

If the block does not measure 3½" x 4½", see Pressing on page 8.

Sew the 4 D blocks into a column by sewing them together along the 4½" side. The block column should measure 4½" x 12½".

COMPLETING THE QUILT

Refer to Finishing Your Quilt on page 46 for directions on making the quilt top, laying out the motifs, and completing your quilt.

Fig. 4

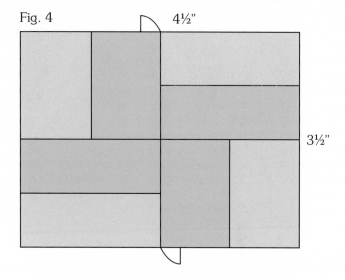

4½"

3½"

Notes on making the motifs:
After you cut the smaller cross, trace the opening and cut out the four-pointed shape.

When you are laying out the crosses, remove the fusible paper from the back of the purple cross; then center it over the cream cross.

If you wish, you can first fuse the two crosses together using the Appliqué Pressing Sheet. By doing this, both crosses become one unit. This makes it easier to move the motif over the quilt when you are deciding on the layout.

Say *Thank You!* as only a quilter can—with a unique quilt that lets the receiver know just how much they are appreciated.

FABRIC AND MATERIALS

- ♥ Light batik - 1 fat quarter
- ♥ Dark batik - 2 fat quarters
- ♥ Backing - 1 fat quarter
- ♥ Felted wool:
    Flower - 13" x 14" orange
    Heart - 2" x 2" red
    Letters and flower stamen -
    10" x 16" yellow
- ♥ Fusible web - 1 yard
- ♥ Fusible batting - one 19" x 20" piece
- ♥ Two plastic rings size ½"
- ♥ Templates (page 49)
    Petals 1 – 5
    Stamen
    Small heart (page 56)
    Alphabet (pages 61 – 62)

CUTTING DIRECTIONS

* Set pieces A, B, C, and E aside while you make the D blocks. Once you have assembled the four 3½" x 4½" D blocks, you will sew the quilt top together.

LIGHT BATIK

Three 1⅞" x 18" strips
One 8½" x 12½" rectangle (C)*

DARK BATIK

Three 1⅞" x 18" strips
One 4" x 15" strip (A)*
One 3" x 12½" strip (B)*
Four 2¼" x 18" strips (E)*

MAKING THE D BLOCKS

Make 2 different strips-sets using the 1⅞" x 18" strips:

Sew 1 light strip between 2 dark strips. Press seams towards the dark fabric.

Sew 1 dark strip between 2 light strips. Press seams towards the dark fabric.

Cut six 1½" segments from each strip-set.

Following figures 1 and 2, lay out and sew the nine-patch blocks. Press. You will have 2 blocks of each color configuration.

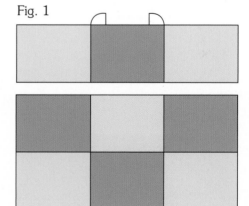

Fig. 1

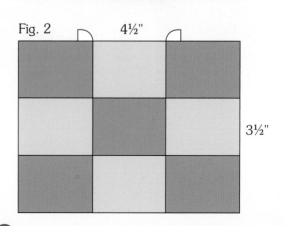

Fig. 2   4½"

3½"

If the block does not measure 3½" x 4½", see Pressing on page 8.

Sew the 4 D blocks into a column by sewing them together along the 4½" side. Alternate the dark center/light center color configurations. The block column should measure 4½" x 12½".

COMPLETING THE QUILT

Refer to Finishing Your Quilt on page 46 for directions on making the quilt top, laying out the motifs, and completing your quilt.

The short lines in the templates denote that the piece overlaps another. For example, template 3 shows that it overlaps pieces 4 and 5.

We recommend using the Appliqué Pressing Sheet when laying out and fusing the flower. It will make it easier to place on the quilt top.

Note on making the motifs:
Lay out the petals in the order shown in figure 3. When laying out the flower, place the flower's stamen over piece #2.

Fig. 3

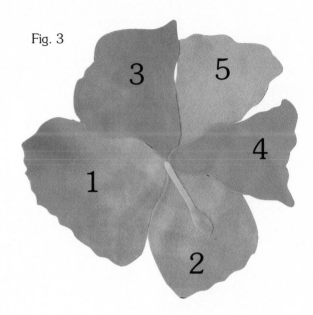

TUTU TERRIFIC

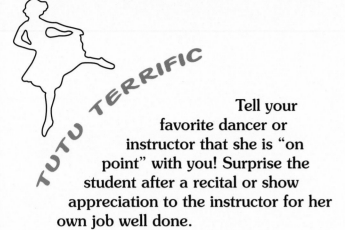

TUTU TERRIFIC

Tell your favorite dancer or instructor that she is "on point" with you! Surprise the student after a recital or show appreciation to the instructor for her own job well done.

FABRIC AND MATERIALS

- ♥ Light batik - 1 fat quarter
- ♥ Dark batik - 2 fat quarters
- ♥ Backing - 1 fat quarter
- ♥ Felted wool:
    Dancer – 10" x 13" fuchsia
    Heart - 2" x 2" red
    Letters and tutu folds - 10" x 16" teal
- ♥ Fusible web - 1 yard
- ♥ Fusible batting - one 19" x 20" piece
- ♥ Two plastic rings size ½"
- ♥ 4 copies of the paper-piecing pattern
- ♥ Templates (page 50)
    Dancer
    Tutu folds
    Small heart (page 56)
    Alphabet (pages 61 – 62)

CUTTING DIRECTIONS

* Set pieces A, B, C, and E aside while you make the D blocks. Once you have assembled the four 3½" x 4½" D blocks, you will sew the quilt top together.

LIGHT BATIK

Two 1½" x 18" strips
    Cut into sixteen 1⅞" x 1½" rectangles
One 1¾" x 18" strip
    Cut into eight 1¾" x 1¾" squares
One 8½" x 12½" rectangle (C)*

DARK BATIK

Two 1½" x 18" strips
    Cut into sixteen 1⅞" x 1½" rectangles
One 1¾" x 18" strip
    Cut into eight 1¾" x 1¾" squares
One 4" x 15" rectangle (A)*
One 3" x 12½" rectangle (B)*
Four 2¼" x 18" strips (E)*

Paper-Piecing Notes:

This block is sewn using both paper pattern and regular piecing techniques. It is recomended that you make all the pattern copies for paper piecing from the same copy machine to avoid distortion.

Before you start paper piecing, trim each paper pattern to approximately ⅛" outside of the cutting (dashed) line. This makes it easier to handle the paper and the fabric together.

Reduce your stitch length whenever you work with paper foundations. It makes it much easier to remove the paper later on.

Remove the paper pattern only after all four blocks have been sewn together into the block border.

MAKING THE D BLOCKS

Lay the paper-piecing pattern printed-side up, onto the back of a dark square.

Lay the paper and dark fabric square on top of the right side of a light square (Fig. 1)

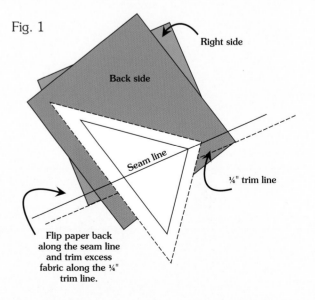

Fig. 1

Right side

Back side

Seam line

¼" trim line

Flip paper back along the seam line and trim excess fabric along the ¼" trim line.

Sew on the seam line.

Fold back the paper pattern back along the seam line and trim any excess fabric, leaving a ¼" allowance. Be careful not to cut the paper pattern.

Open the fabric along the seam (Fig. 2). Press.

Fig. 2

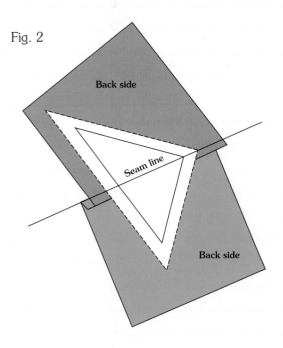

Using the ruler and rotary cutter, trim along the cutting (dashed) line. Leave the paper in place.

Repeat to make a total of 4 paper-pieced triangles with this color configuration (Fig. 3).

Fig. 3

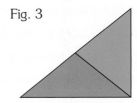

Now make 4 paper-pieced triangles the same way, using 4 light and 4 dark squares but reversing the color placement (Fig. 4).

Fig. 4

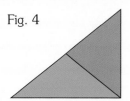

Lay out 2 paper-pieced triangles according to figure 5.

Fig. 5

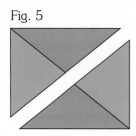

Flip the top piece over the bottom piece, aligning the long edge (Fig. 6).

Fig. 6

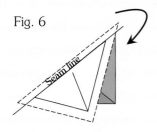

Pin the corners, the center, and along the seam line. Make sure that the seam lines on both patterns are perfectly aligned.

Sew on the seam line. Press the seam open. This reduces the bulk, allowing the block to lie flatter. Do not remove the paper yet. However, you may carefully remove the small paper strip on the seam line so that small pieces of paper will not get caught between the seams.

Repeat to make a total of 2 rectangles with this color configuration (Fig. 7) and 2 rectangles of the opposite configuration (Fig. 8).

Fig. 7

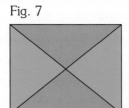

Fig. 8

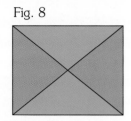

Follow figure 9 and lay out the 4 blocks, using the pieced center rectangles and the cut 1⅞" x 1½" rectangles. You will have 2 blocks of each color configuration. (Shown here is only one configuration.)

Assemble each block by sewing each rectangle into columns.

Fig. 9

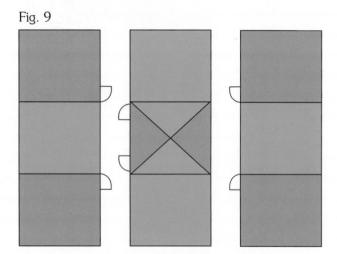

Sew the columns together (Fig. 10). Press to the dark fabric, taking as reference the corner rectangles.

Note: If you press the seams to the dark fabric using the corner pieces as guidelines, the seams will naturally "oppose" when you lay out the 4½" x 12½" column.

Fig. 10

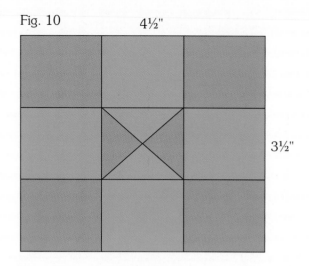

4½"

3½"

If the block does not measure 3½" x 4½", see Pressing on page 8.

Sew the 4 D blocks into a column by sewing along the 4½" side and alternating color configurations. The block column should measure 4½" x 12½".

Remove the paper.

COMPLETING THE QUILT

Refer to Finishing Your Quilt on page 46 for directions on making the quilt top, laying out the motifs, and completing your quilt.

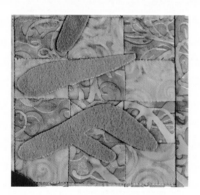

YOU SHINE

A good teacher can inspire our children to dream and to become. If your child is lucky enough to have a strong mentor or role model, honor that person with a shining star of his or her own!

FABRIC AND MATERIALS

- ♥ Light batik - 1 fat quarter
- ♥ Dark batik - 2 fat quarters
- ♥ Backing - 1 fat quarter
- ♥ Felted wool:
    Star - 11" x 15" yellow
    Heart - 2" x 2" red
    Letters - 10" x 16" orange
- ♥ Fusible web - 1 yard
- ♥ Fusible batting - one 19" x 20" piece
- ♥ Two plastic rings size ½"
- ♥ 4 copies of the paper-piecing pattern
- ♥ Templates (page 51)
    Star
    Small heart (page 56)
    Alphabet (pages 61 – 62)

CUTTING DIRECTIONS

* Set pieces A, B, C, and E aside while you make the D blocks. Once you have assembled the four 3½" x 4½" D blocks, you will sew the quilt top together.

LIGHT BATIK

Two 3¼" x 18" strips
    Cut into eight 4" x 3¼" rectangles
One 8½" x 12½" rectangle (C)*

DARK BATIK

Two 3¼" x 18" strips
    Cut into eight 4" x 3¼" rectangles
One 4" x 15" rectangle (A)*

One 3" x 12½" rectangle (B)*
Four 2¼" x 18" strips (E)*

Paper-Piecing Notes:

This block is sewn using both paper pattern and regular piecing techniques. It is recomended that you make all the pattern copies for paper piecing from the same copy machine to avoid distortion.

Before you start paper piecing, trim each paper pattern to approximately ⅛" outside of the cutting (dashed) line. This makes it easier to handle the paper and the fabric together.

Reduce your stitch length whenever you work with paper foundations. It makes it much easier to remove the paper later on.

Remove the paper pattern only after all four blocks have been sewn together into the block border.

MAKING THE D BLOCKS

Follow figure 1 and lay the paper pattern printed-side up onto the wrong side of a dark rectangle.

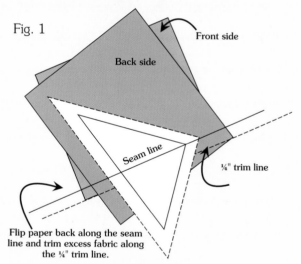

Fig. 1

Front side

Back side

Seam line

¼" trim line

Flip paper back along the seam line and trim excess fabric along the ¼" trim line.

Lay the paper and fabric on top of the right side of a light rectangle.

Sew on the seam line.

Flip the paper pattern back along the seam line and trim any excess fabric, leaving a ¼" allowance. Be careful not to cut the paper pattern.

Open the fabric along the seam (Fig. 2). Press.

Fig. 2

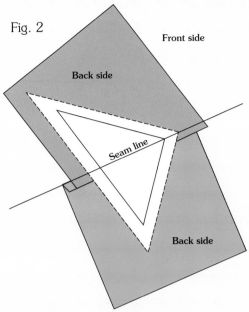

Using the ruler and rotary cutter, trim along the cutting (dashed) line.

Repeat to make a total of 4 paper-pieced triangles with this color configuration (Fig. 3).

Fig. 3

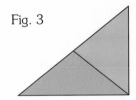

Now make 4 paper-pieced triangles using the remaining 4 light 4" x 3¼" rectangles and 4 dark 4" x 3¼" rectangles but reverse the color placement.

Lay out 2 paper-pieced triangles according to figure 4.

Fig. 4

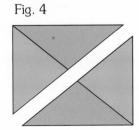

Flip the top piece over the bottom piece, aligning the long edge (Fig. 5). Pin the corners, the center, and along the seam line. Make sure that the seam lines on both patterns are perfectly aligned.

Fig. 5

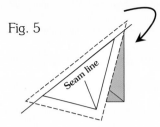

Sew on the seam line. Press the seam open. This reduces the bulk, allowing the block to lie flatter.

Repeat to make a total of 4 blocks. You will have 2 blocks with this color configuration and 2 blocks of the opposite configuration.

If the block does not measure 3½" x 4½", see Pressing on page 8.

Sew the 4 blocks into a column by sewing along the 4½" side. The block column should measure 4½" x 12½". Make any adjustments if necessary.

Fig. 6   4½"

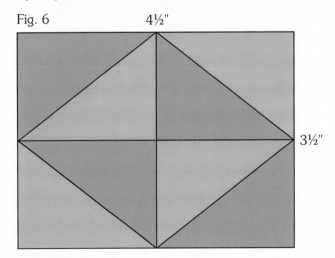

3½"

Remove the paper.

COMPLETING THE QUILT

Refer to Finishing Your Quilt on page 46 for directions on making the quilt top, laying out the motifs, and completing your quilt.

Some teachers guide and instruct our children in the wonderful worlds of music and art. Be grateful for that extraordinary creative guide and show him or her just how much you appreciate their work!

FABRIC AND MATERIALS

- ♥ Light batik - 1 fat quarter
- ♥ Dark batik - 2 fat quarters
- ♥ Backing - 1 fat quarter
- ♥ Felted wool:
     G clef - 8" x 14" black
     Heart - 2" x 2" red
     Letters - 10" x 16" orange
- ♥ Fusible web - 1 yard
- ♥ Fusible batting - one 19" x 20" piece
- ♥ Two plastic rings size ½"
- ♥ Templates (page 52)
     G Clef
     Small heart (page 56)
     Alphabet (pages 61 – 62)

CUTTING DIRECTIONS

* Set pieces A, B, C, and E aside while you make the D blocks. Once you have assembled the four 3½" x 4½" D blocks, you will sew the quilt top together.

LIGHT BATIK

One 8½" x 12½" rectangle C*
Two 2¾" x 18" strips
   Cut into eight 3½" x 2¾" rectangles.

Place rectangles right-side up and divide into 2 stacks of 4 rectangles.

> *Note:* It is very important to stack the rectangles right-side up. If any of the pieces are lying face down, the cut triangles will not fit correctly when you sew the pieced rectangles.

Cut one stack in half, corner to corner, following figure 1. Label as L-A triangles.

Cut the second stack in half, corner to corner, following figure 2. Label as L-B triangles.

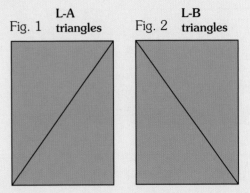

Fig. 1 L-A triangles   Fig. 2 L-B triangles

Mark a ¼" seam allowance along the long, wrong side of all light triangles.

DARK BATIK

One 4" x 15" rectangle (A)*
One 3" x 12½" rectangle (B)*
Four 2¼" x 18" strips (E)*
Two 2¾" x 18" strips
   Cut into eight 3½" x 2¾" rectangles.

Follow the steps for the light batik to cut rectangles in half, corner to corner. Label them as D-A and D-B, depending on which figure (1 or 2) was used to cut them.

MAKING THE D BLOCKS

Using L-A and D-A triangles, place a light triangle over a dark one, right sides together, and align the long side of both triangles (Fig. 3).

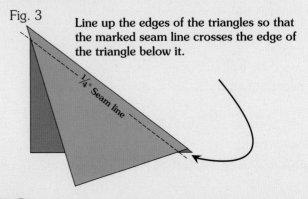

Fig. 3

Line up the edges of the triangles so that the marked seam line crosses the edge of the triangle below it.

¼" Seam line

Sew. Press towards the dark triangle.

Trim down to 2" x 2½" (Fig. 4).

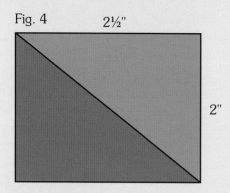

Fig. 4   2½"

2"

Repeat with the remaining L-A and D-A triangles to make a total of eight 2" x 2½" pieced rectangles.

Repeat with the L-B and D-B triangles to make a total of eight 2" x 2½" pieced rectangles.

Following figure 5, assemble each block.

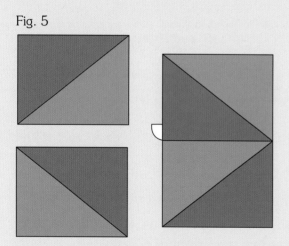

Fig. 5

Repeat to make a total of four 3½" x 4½" blocks as shown in figure 6.

If the block does not measure 3½" x 4½", see Pressing on page 8.

Sew the 4 blocks into a column by sewing along the 4½" side. The block column should measure 4½" x 12½".

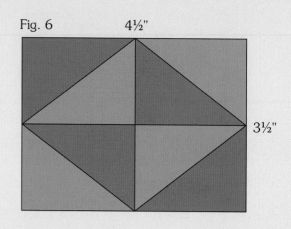

Fig. 6   4½"

3½"

COMPLETING THE QUILT

Refer to Finishing Your Quilt on page 46 for directions on making the quilt top, laying out the motifs, and completing your quilt.

Nurses, doctors, and medical professionals of many kinds bring us joy and hope during difficult times. Show them what their expert, loving care means to you and your family with this quilt.

FABRIC AND MATERIALS

- ♥ Light batik - 1 fat quarter
- ♥ Dark batik - 2 fat quarters
- ♥ Backing - 1 fat quarter
- ♥ Felted wool:
     Sun - 11" x 12" yellow
     Heart - 2" x 2" red
     Letters - 10" x 16" plaid
     Spiral - 8" x 8" orange
- ♥ Fusible web - 1 yard
- ♥ Fusible batting - one 19" x 20" piece
- ♥ Two plastic rings size ½"
- ♥ Templates (page 53)
     Sun
     Spiral
     Small heart (page 56)
     Alphabet (pages 61 – 62)

CUTTING DIRECTIONS

* Set pieces A, B, C, and E aside while you make the D blocks. Once you have assembled the four 3½" x 4½" D blocks, you will sew the quilt top together.

LIGHT BATIK

One 2½" x 18" strip
     Cut into eight 2" x 2½" rectangles
One 8½" x 12½" rectangle (C)*

DARK BATIK

One 2½" x 18" strip
     Cut into eight 2" x 2½" rectangles
One 1½" x 18" strip
     Cut into eight 1½" squares
One 4" x 15" rectangle (A)*
One 3" x 12½" rectangle (B)*
Four 2¼" x 18" strips (E)*

MAKING THE D BLOCKS

Draw a diagonal line, corner to corner, on the back of all the 1½" squares (Fig. 1). This will be the seam line.

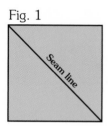

Fig. 1

Lay a marked 1½" square on the top right corner of a light 2" x 2½" rectangle with right sides together. Align the seam line according to figure 2.

Sew on the drawn line.

Trim ¼" from seam line to remove excess fabric (Fig. 2).

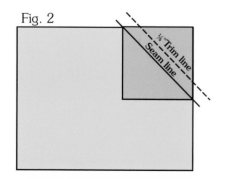

Fig. 2

Press to the dark fabric.

Repeat to make a total of 8 units (Fig. 3).

Fig. 3

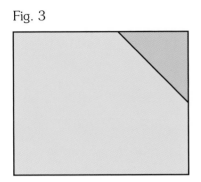

Following figure 4, lay out and assemble the block.

Fig. 4

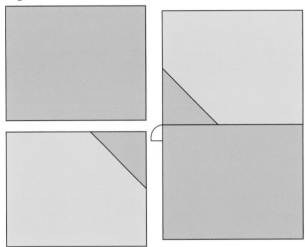

If the block does not measure 3½" x 4½", see Pressing on page 8.

Repeat to make a total of four 3½" x 4½" blocks (Fig. 5).

Fig. 5   4½"

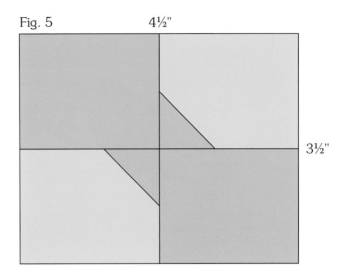

3½"

Sew the 4 blocks into a column by sewing along the 4½" side. Press the seam of 2 of the blocks in one direction and 2 blocks in the opposite direction. Alternate directions when sewing the blocks into a column. The block column should measure 4½" x 12½".

COMPLETING THE QUILT

Refer to Finishing Your Quilt on page 46 for directions on making the quilt top, laying out the motifs, and completing your quilt.

YOU ARE LOVED

You say it, and now you can show it. Remind that special someone just how much they are cared for. Remember—you do not need a reason to say Thanks, I love you!

FABRIC AND MATERIALS

♥ Light batik - 1 fat quarter
♥ Dark batik - 2 fat quarters
♥ Backing - 1 fat quarter
♥ Felted wool:
    Big heart - 11" x 11" burgundy
    Small heart - 2" x 2" red
    Letters - 10" x 16" plaid
♥ Fusible web - 1 yard
♥ Fusible batting - one 19" x 20" piece
♥ Two plastic rings size ½"
♥ Templates (page 54)
    Big heart
    Small heart (page 56)
    Alphabet (pages 61 – 62)

CUTTING DIRECTIONS

* Set pieces A, B, C, and E aside while you make the D blocks. Once you have assembled the four 3½" x 4½" D blocks, you will sew the quilt top together.

LIGHT BATIK

One 2¼" x 18" strip.
    Cut into six 3" x 2¼" rectangles.

Note: It is very important to stack the rectangles right-side up. If any of the pieces are laying face down, the cut triangles will not fit correctly when sewing the pieced rectangles.

Lay rectangles right-side up and divide into 2 stacks of 3 rectangles.
    Cut each stack in half, corner to corner, following figure 1.
    Mark a ¼" seam allowance along the long, back side of all light triangles.
    One 3¾" x 18" strip. (You'll have 8" left over, so cut the strip 10" long if you prefer.)
    Cut into two 5" x 3¾" rectangles.
Lay both rectangles right-side up and cut in half, following figure 1.
One 8½" x 12½" rectangle (C)*

DARK BATIK

One 4" x 15" rectangle (A)*
One 3" x 12½" rectangle (B)*
Four 2¼" x 18" strips (E)*
Two 2¼" x 18" strips
    Cut into twelve 2¼" x 3" rectangles.
Lay the rectangles right-side up and divide into 3 stacks of 4 rectangles.
    Cut each stack in half, corner to corner, following figure 1.

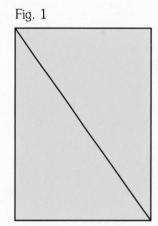

Fig. 1

Trim twelve of the triangles to 1⅞" x 1½" (Fig. 2). Set aside.

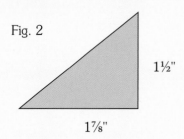

Fig. 2

1½"

1⅞"

YOU ARE LOVED

MAKING THE D BLOCKS

Place a light triangle over a dark 3" x 2¼" triangle with right sides together, aligning the long side of both triangles (Fig. 3).

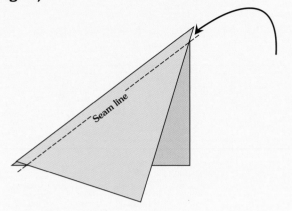

Sew. Press towards the dark triangle.

Trim to 1½" x 1⅞" (Fig. 4).

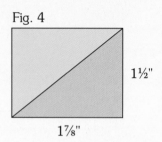

Fig. 4

1½"

1⅞"

Repeat to make a total of twelve 1½" x 1⅞" pieced rectangles.

Following figure 5, assemble the triangles and pieced rectangles.

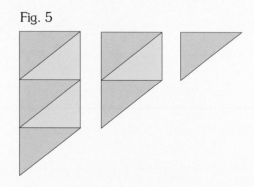

Fig. 5

Repeat to make 4 pieced triangles.

Sew a pieced triangle to the larger light fabric triangle (Fig. 6). Press towards the large triangle.

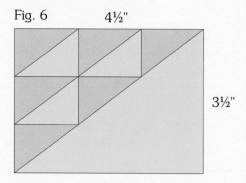

Fig. 6   4½"

3½"

Repeat to make a total of four a 3½" x 4½" blocks.

If the block does not measure 3½" x 4½", see Pressing on page 8.

Sew the 4 blocks into a column by sewing along the 4½" side. The block column should measure 4½" x 12½".

COMPLETING THE QUILT

Refer to Finishing Your Quilt on page 46 for directions on making the quilt top, laying out the motifs, and completing your quilt.

> **Note on making the motifs:**
> The large heart is all one piece. When you are laying it on the quilt top, make sure that the edges right over the cutout are touching. This area is clearly marked in the template.

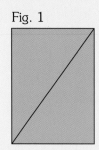

WARM WISHES

Like a great cup of coffee, let someone know that you look forward to seeing them or that you wish them the best in their endeavors. Send them "Warm Wishes" that will be cherished for a lifetime.

FABRIC AND MATERIALS

- ♥ Light batik - 1 fat quarter
- ♥ Dark batik - 2 fat quarters
- ♥ Backing - 1 fat quarter
- ♥ Felted wool:
    Mug body - 10" x 10" light teal
    Mug opening - 4" x 8" dark teal
    Steam - 3½" x 6" white
    Heart - 2" x 2" red
    Letters - 10" x 16" plaid
- ♥ Fusible web - 1 yard
- ♥ Fusible batting - one 19" x 20" piece
- ♥ Two plastic rings size ½"
- ♥ Templates (page 55)
    Mug body
    Mug opening
    Steam
    Small heart (page 56)
    Alphabet (pages 61 – 62)

CUTTING DIRECTIONS

* Set pieces A, B, C, and E aside while you make the D blocks. Once you have assembled the four 3½" x 4½" D blocks, you will sew the quilt top together.

LIGHT BATIK

Two 2¼" x 18" strips
    Cut into eight 3" x 2¼" rectangles and four 1⅞" x 1½" rectangles.
    Place all 3" x 2¼" rectangles right-side up and divide into 2 stacks of 4 rectangles.
    Cut each stack in half, corner to corner, following Figure 1.

Fig. 1

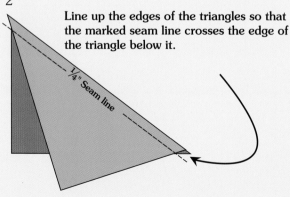

Mark a ¼" seam allowance along the long, back side of all light triangles.
One 1¾" x 18" strip
    Cut into eight 1¾" x 1¾" squares.
One 8½" x 12½" rectangle (C)*

> **Note:** Stacking and cutting more than four rectangles at a time may reduce your cutting accuracy. You may want to cut each of them individually.

DARK BATIK

Two 2¼" x 18" strips
    Cut into eight 3" x 2¼" rectangles.
Follow the steps for the light batik and cut the rectangles in half corner to corner.
Two 1½" x 18" strips
    Cut into sixteen 1⅞" x 1½" rectangles.
One 4" x 15" rectangle (A)*
One 3" x 12½" rectangle (B)*
Four 2¼" x 18" strips (E)*

MAKING THE D BLOCKS

Place a light triangle over a dark triangle with right sides together, aligning the long side of both triangles (Fig. 2).

Fig. 2

Line up the edges of the triangles so that the marked seam line crosses the edge of the triangle below it.

¼" Seam line

Trim down to 1⅞" x 1½" (Fig.3).

To make the stem rectangle, draw a diagonal line, corner to corner, on the back of all 1¾" x 1¾" light squares (Fig. 4). Repeat to make 16 pieced rectangles.

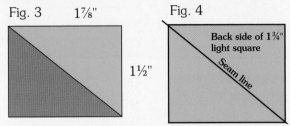

Fig. 3   1⅞"

1½"

Fig. 4

Back side of 1¾" light square

Seam line

Place a 1¾" x 1¾" marked square on top of a 1⅞" x 1½" dark rectangle with right sides together, aligning the lower left corner of both pieces. Align the marked line according to figure 5.

Sew on the marked line.

Cut on the ¼" trim line (Fig. 5) to remove excess fabric. Press open (Fig. 6).

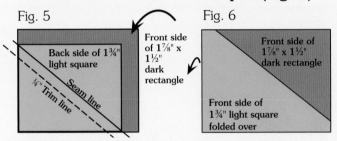

Fig. 5

Back side of 1¾" light square

¼" Trim line

Seam line

Front side of 1⅞" x 1½" dark rectangle

Fig. 6

Front side of 1⅞" x 1½" dark rectangle

Front side of 1¾" light square folded over

Place a second 1¾" x 1¾" marked square on top of the 1⅞" x 1½" dark rectangle right sides together, aligning the upper right corner of both pieces. Align the marked seam line according to figure 7 and sew.

Cut on the ¼" trim line (Fig. 7) to remove excess fabric. Press open (Fig. 8).

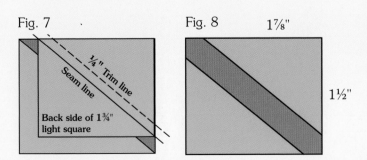

Fig. 7

¼" Trim line

Seam line

Back side of 1¾" light square

Fig. 8   1⅞"

1½"

If necessary, trim the rectangle to 1⅞" x 1½". Repeat to make a total of 4 blocks.

Follow figure 9 to assemble the blocks. Repeat to make a total of four 3½" x 4½" blocks.

If the block does not measure 3½" x 4½", see Pressing on page 8.

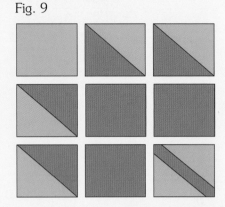

Fig. 9

Sew the 4 blocks into a column by sewing along the 4½" side. The block column should measure 4½" x 12½".

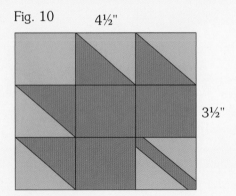

Fig. 10   4½"

3½"

COMPLETING THE QUILT

Refer to Finishing Your Quilt on page 46 for directions on making the quilt top, laying out the motifs, and completing your quilt.

Notes on making the motif:
Follow the register lines drawn in the templates to lay out the dark opening of the mug over its body. Do the same with the seam piece.

There is nothing like a true friend! On a bad day, she is there to cheer you up, and on a good day she shares the moment in full. Say Thanks! to this special friend with a quilt just for her – your True Friend!

FABRIC AND MATERIALS

- ♥ Light batik - 1 fat quarter
- ♥ Dark batik - 2 fat quarters
- ♥ Backing - 1 fat quarter
- ♥ Felted wool:
     Glove - 9" x 14" brown
     Large hearts - three 4" x 4" pink
     Heart - 2" x 2" red
     Letters - 10" x 16" pink
- ♥ Fusible web - 1 yard
- ♥ Fusible batting - one 19" x 20" piece
- ♥ Two plastic rings size ½"
- ♥ Templates (page 56)
     Glove
     Large heart
     Small heart
     Alphabet (pages 61 – 62)

CUTTING DIRECTIONS

* Set pieces A, B, C, and E aside while you make the D blocks. Once you have assembled the four 3½" x 4½" D blocks, you will sew the quilt top together.

LIGHT BATIK

Two 2¼" x 18" strips

Cut into eight 3" x 2¼" rectangles and four 1⅞" x 1½" rectangles. Set aside the 1⅞" x 1½" rectangles.

Lay all 3" x 2¼" rectangles right-side up and divide into 2 stacks of 4 rectangles.

Cut one stack in half, corner to corner, following figure 1. Label as L-A triangles.
Cut the second stack in half corner to corner, following figure 2. Label as L-B triangles.

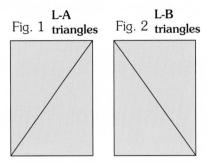

Fig. 1 L-A triangles   Fig. 2 L-B triangles

Mark a ¼" seam allowance along the long, back side of all light triangles.
One 8½" x 12½" rectangle (C)*

DARK BATIK

Two 2¼" x 18" strips
     Cut into eight 3" x 2¼" rectangles.

Follow the steps for the light batik and cut the rectangles in half corner to corner.
Label them as D-A and D-B, depending on which figure was used to cut them.

Two 1½" x 18" strips
     Cut into sixteen 1⅞" x 1½" rectangles.
One 4" x 15" rectangle (A)*
One 3" x 12½" rectangle (B)*
Four 2¼" x 18" strips (E)*

MAKING THE D BLOCKS

Using L-A and D-A triangles, place a light triangle over a dark triangle with right sides together, aligning the long side of both triangles (Fig. 3).

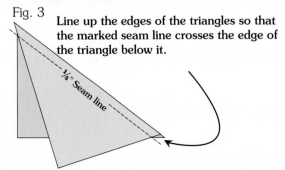

Fig. 3   Line up the edges of the triangles so that the marked seam line crosses the edge of the triangle below it.
¼" Seam line

Sew. Press towards the dark triangle.

Trim down to 1⅞" x 1½" (Fig. 4).

Repeat with the remaining L-A and D-A triangles to make a total of 8 pieced rectangles. Label as "A" pieced rectangles.

Repeat with the L-B and D-B triangles to make a total of eight 1⅞" x 1½" pieced rectangles (Fig. 5). Label as "B" pieced rectangles.

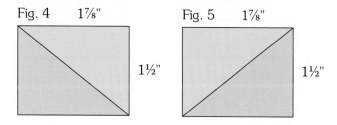

Fig. 4   1⅞"   1½"   Fig. 5   1⅞"   1½"

Following figure 6, assemble the blocks.

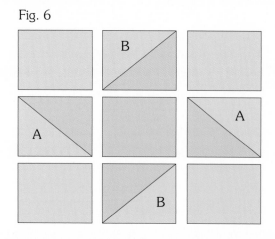

Fig. 6

Sew the rectangles in columns (Fig. 7). Press.

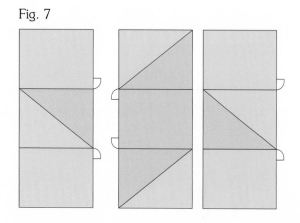

Fig. 7

Sew the columns together (Fig. 8). Press.

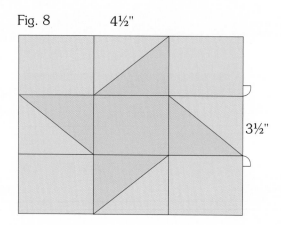

Fig. 8   4½"   3½"

Repeat to make a total of four 3½" x 4½" blocks.

If the block does not measure 3½" x 4½", see Pressing on page 8.

Sew the 4 blocks into a column by sewing along the 4½" side. The block column should measure 4½" x 12 ½".

> **Note on making the motifs:**
> Follow the register lines drawn in the templates to lay out the 3 hearts over the glove.

COMPLETING THE QUILT

Refer to Finishing Your Quilt on page 46 for directions on making the quilt top, laying out the motifs, and completing your quilt.

A winning touchdown, a goal achieved, or a season of personal bests… recognize the athlete or extraordinary coach with this special celebration quilt.

FABRIC AND MATERIALS

- ♥ Light batik - 1 fat quarter
- ♥ Dark batik - 2 fat quarters
- ♥ Backing - 1 fat quarter
- ♥ Felted wool:
    Football's base and seam -
  12" x 13" cream
    Football parts - 9" x 14" brown
    Heart - 2" x 2" red
    Letters - 10" x 16" plaid
- ♥ Fusible web - 1 yard
- ♥ Fusible batting - one 19" x 20" piece
- ♥ Two plastic rings size ½"
- ♥ Templates (page 57)
    Football base
    Football point 1
    Football point 2
    Football body
    Seam
    Small heart (page 56)
    Alphabet (pages 61 – 62)

CUTTING DIRECTIONS

* Set pieces A, B, C, and E aside while you make the D blocks. Once you have assembled the four 3½" x 4½" D blocks, you will sew the quilt top together.

LIGHT BATIK

Two 2¼" x 18" strips
    Cut into eight 3" x 2¼" rectangles.
Place the rectangles right-side up and divide them into 2 stacks of 4 rectangles.
    Cut one stack in half, corner to corner, following figure 1. Label as L-A triangles.
    Cut the second stack in half, corner to corner, following figure 2. Label as L-B triangles.

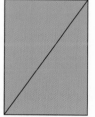

Fig. 1   L-A triangles   Fig. 2   L-B triangles

Mark a ¼" seam allowance along the long, back side of all light triangles.
Two 1⅞" x 18" strips
    Cut into ten 1⅞" x 1½" rectangles.
One 8½" x 12½" rectangle (C)*

DARK BATIK

Two 2¼" x 18" strips
    Cut into eight 3" x 2¼" rectangles.

Follow the steps for the light batik and cut the rectangles in half, corner to corner. Label them as D-A and D-B, depending on which figure (1 or 2) was used to cut them.

Two 1⅞" x 18" strips
    Cut into ten 1⅞" x 1½" rectangles.
One 4" x 15" rectangle (A)*
One 3" x 12½" rectangle (B)*
Four 2¼" x 18" strips (E)*

MAKING THE D BLOCKS

Using L-A and D-A triangles, place a light triangle over a dark triangle, right sides together, aligning the long side of both triangles (Fig. 3).

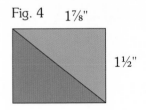

Fig. 3

Line up the edges of the triangles so that the marked seam line crosses the edge of the triangle below it.

¼" Seam line

Sew. Press towards the dark triangle.

Trim down to 1⅞" x 1½" (Fig. 4). Label as "A" pieced rectangles.

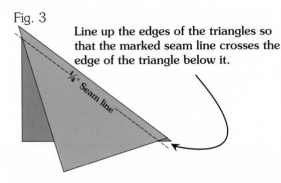

Fig. 4   1⅞"

1½"

Repeat to make a total of eight 1⅞" x 1½" pieced "A" rectangles.

Repeat with the L-B and D-B triangles to make a total of eight 1⅞" x 1½" pieced rectangles. Label as "B" pieced rectangles.

Following figure 5, assemble the blocks. Two blocks should follow the dark center layout and 2 blocks the light center layout. Figure 5 shows the dark center layout.

Note on making the motifs:
Follow the register lines drawn in the templates to lay out the parts of the football over the football base. Repeat with the seam piece. Using the Appliqué Pressing Sheet helps when placing and fusing these motifs.

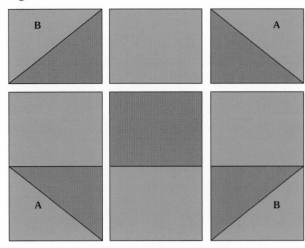

Fig. 5

Press. Blocks with a dark center rectangle should be pressed towards the center (Fig. 5). Those with a light center rectangle should be pressed away from the center (Fig. 6).

If the block does not measure 3½" x 4½", see Pressing on page 8.

Sew the 4 blocks into a column by sewing along the 4½" side and alternating the 2 different color configurations. The block column should measure 4½" x 12½".

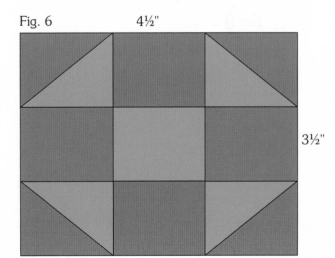

Fig. 6   4½"

3½"

COMPLETING THE QUILT

Refer to Finishing Your Quilt on page 46 for directions on making the quilt top, laying out the motifs, and completing your quilt.

Your pet is a special member of the family. Let your vets know much you appreciate their care and attention to this beloved four-legged friend.

FABRIC AND MATERIALS

- ♥ Light batik - 1 fat quarter
- ♥ Dark batik - 2 fat quarters
- ♥ Backing - 1 fat quarter
- ♥ Felted wool:
     Cat - 9" x 12½" navy blue
     Heart - 2" x 2" red
     Letters - 10" x 16" plaid
- ♥ Fusible web - 1 yard
- ♥ Fusible batting - one 19" x 20" piece
- ♥ Two plastic rings size ½"
- ♥ Templates (page 58)
     Cat
     Small heart (page 56)
     Alphabet (pages 61 – 62)

CUTTING DIRECTIONS

* Set pieces A, B, C, and E aside while you make the D blocks. Once you have assembled the four 3½" x 4½" D blocks, you will sew the quilt top together.

LIGHT BATIK

Two 3" x 18" strips
     Cut into eight 2½" x 3" rectangles.

Place rectangles right-side up and divide into 2 stacks of 4 rectangles.

Cut one stack in half, corner to corner, following figure 1. Label as L-A triangles.

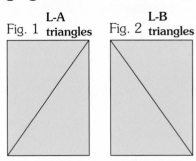

Cut the second stack in half, corner to corner, following figure 2. Label as L-B triangles.

Mark a ¼" seam allowance along the long, wrong side of all light triangles.
     One 1¼" x 18" strip
          Cut into four 1¼" x 1¼" squares.
     One 8½" x 12½" rectangle (C)*

Note: It is very important to stack the rectangles right-side up. If any of the pieces are lying face down, the cut triangles will not fit correctly when you sew the pieced rectangles.

DARK BATIK

Two 3" x 18" strips
     Cut into eight 2½" x 3" rectangles.

Follow the steps for the light batik and cut the rectangles in half, corner to corner. Label them as D-A and D-B, depending on which figure was used to cut them.

Two 1¼" x 18" strips
     Cut into eight 1⅝" x 1¼" rectangles and eight 2⅛" x 1¼" rectangles.
One 4" x 15" rectangle (A)*
One 3" x 12½" rectangle (B)*
Four 2¼" x 18" strips (E)*

LOVE MY VET

MAKING THE D BLOCKS

Using L-A and D-A triangles, place a light triangle over a dark triangle right sides together, aligning the long side of both triangles (Fig. 3).

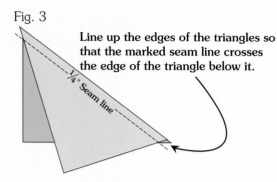

Fig. 3

Line up the edges of the triangles so that the marked seam line crosses the edge of the triangle below it.

¼" Seam line

Sew. Press towards the dark triangle.

Trim rectangles down to 1⅝" x 2⅛" (Fig. 4). Label as "A" pieced rectangles.

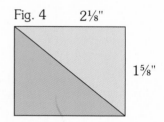

Fig. 4   2⅛"

1⅝"

Repeat to make a total of eight 1⅝" x 2⅛" pieced "A" rectangles.

Repeat with the L-B and D-B triangles to make a total of eight 1⅝" x 2⅛" pieced rectangles (Fig. 5). Label as "B" pieced rectangles

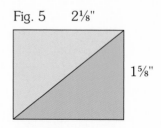

Fig. 5   2⅛"

1⅝"

Following figure 6, assemble the blocks.

Fig. 6

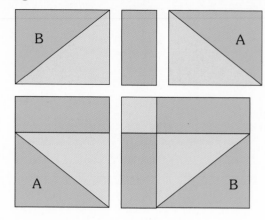

B   A

A   B

Press.

Repeat to make a total of four 3½" x 4½" blocks.

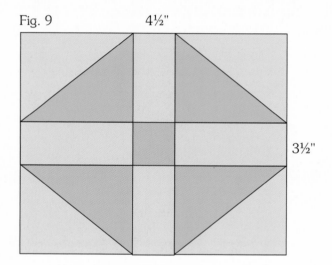

Fig. 9   4½"

3½"

Sew the 4 blocks into a column by sewing along the 4½" side. The block column should measure 4½" x 12½".

COMPLETING THE QUILT

Refer to Finishing Your Quilt on page 46 for directions on making the quilt top, laying out the motifs, and completing your quilt.

Note:
When we designed the cat for LOVE MY VET, we knew dog lovers would want to make this quilt, too!
So, we designed a very cute dog to match our lovely feline. The dog pattern in the template gallery takes the same amount of fabric. (But cats and dogs really aren't alike.)

BLESS THIS HOUSE

BLESS THIS HOUSE

Celebrate the joy of a new house—or let someone know that their home is always a warm, welcoming haven. There are so many reasons to be thankful for a warm and loving home!

FABRIC AND MATERIALS

- ♥ Light batik -1 fat quarter
- ♥ Dark batik - 2 fat quarters
- ♥ Backing - 1 fat quarter
- ♥ Felted wool:
  House - 8" x 11" blue plaid
  Door - 5" x 5" red
  Door knob - purple scrap from the roof
  Roof - 7" x 10" purple
  Heart - 2" x 2" red or a scrap piece from the door
  Letters - 10" x 16" blue
- ♥ Fusible web - 1 yard
- ♥ Fusible batting - one 19" x 20" piece
- ♥ Two plastic rings size ½"
- ♥ Templates (page 60)
  House, Door, Door knob, Roof, Windows, Small heart (page 56)
  Alphabet (pages 61 – 62)

CUTTING DIRECTIONS

* Set pieces A, B, C, and E aside while you make the D blocks. Once you have the (4) 3½" x 4½" D blocks, you will use these pieces to sew the quilt top together.

LIGHT BATIK

Two 2¼" x 18" strip
    Cut into eight 3" x 2¼" rectangles.
Place the rectangles right-side up and divide them into 2 stacks of 4 rectangles.
    Cut one stack in half, corner to corner, following figure 1. Label as L-A triangles.
    Cut the second stack in half, corner to corner, following figure 2. Label as L-B triangles.

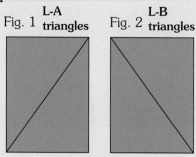

Fig. 1 L-A triangles   Fig. 2 L-B triangles

Mark a ¼" seam allowance along the long, back side of all of the light triangles.
    One 1½" x 18" strip
        Cut into two 1⅞" x 1½" rectangles.
    Trim the remaining strip down to 1¼" wide.
    One 1" x 18" strip
    One 8½" x 12½" rectangle (C)*

DARK BATIK

Two 2¼" x 18" strips
    Cut into eight 3" x 2¼" rectangles.
Follow the steps for the light batik and cut the rectangles in half. Label them as D-A and D-B, depending on which figure was used to cut them.
    One 1½" x 18" strip
        Cut into two 1⅞" x 1½" rectangles.
    Trim the remaining strip down to 1¼" wide.
    One 1" x 18" strip
    One 4" x 15" rectangle (A)*
    One 3" x 12½" rectangle (B)*
    Four 2¼" x 18" strips (E)*

MAKING THE D BLOCKS

Using L-A and D-A triangles, place a light triangle over a dark triangle, right sides together, aligning the long side of both triangles (Fig. 3).

Fig. 3   Line up the edges of the triangles so that the marked seam line crosses the edge of the triangle below it.

¼" Seam line

Sew. Press towards the dark triangle.

Trim down to 1⅞" x 1½" (Fig. 4).

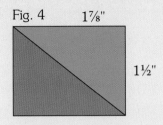

Fig. 4   1⅞"

1½"

Repeat to make a total of eight 1⅞" x 1½" pieced rectangles. Label as "A" pieced rectangles.

Repeat with the L-B and D-B triangles to make a total of eight 1⅞" x 1½" pieced rectangles. Label as "B" pieced rectangles.

Make a 1½" wide strip-set by sewing the light 1" x 18" strip to the dark 1" x 18" strip. Press to the dark fabric.

Cut the strip-set into eight 1⅞" x 1½" rectangles (Fig. 5). Label as "C" rectangles.

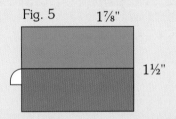

Fig. 5   1⅞"

1½"

Make a 2" wide strip-set by sewing the light 1¼" trimmed strip to the dark 1¼" trimmed strip. Press to the dark fabric.

Cut the strip-set into eight 1½" x 2" rectangles (Fig. 6). Label as "D" rectangles.

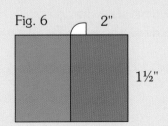

Fig. 6   2"

1½"

Following figure 7, assemble the blocks. Make 2 blocks with the dark center layout and 2 blocks with the light center layout. Shown here is the dark center layout.

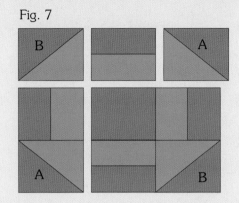

Fig. 7

B   A

A   B

Note: D rectangles are ⅛" wider than required. When laying out the blocks, align the D rectangles with the inside edges of the blocks on top and below. Any excess fabric will stick out on the outside edge and can be easily trimmed when squaring the block.

Blocks with a dark center rectangle should be pressed towards the center. Those with a light center rectangle should be pressed away from the center.

If the block does not measure 3½" x 4½", see Pressing on page 8.

Sew the 4 blocks into a column by sewing along the 4½" side and alternating the 2 different color configurations. The block column should measure 4½" x 12½".

COMPLETING THE QUILT

Refer to Finishing Your Quilt on page 46 for directions on making the quilt top, laying out the motifs, and completing your quilt.

This project really benefits from using the Appliqué Pressing Sheet!

FINISHING YOUR QUILT

PUTTING THE QUILT TOP TOGETHER

Now that you have all the D blocks sewn together and the A, B, and C pieces cut, you are ready to piece your quilt top!

Make sure the 4-block D column measures 4½" x 12½". Make any adjustments if necessary.

Sew the D column to the 8½" x 12½" base (C). Press toward C (Fig. 1).

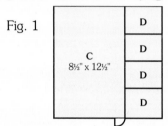

Fig. 1

Sew the 3" x 12½" border (B) to the sewn base (C) and block border (D), following figure 2. Press towards B.

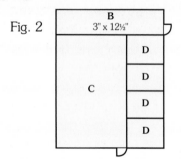

Fig. 2

Sew the 4" x 15" border (A) to the B/C/D sewn pieces (Fig. 3). Press towards A.
And with this, your quilt top is ready!

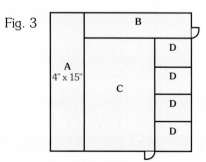

Fig. 3

Wasn't that easy? Now, let's quilt before we go have fun with the wool.

QUILTING AND BINDING THE QUILT TOP

Square the quilt top. It should measure 15" x 16".

To make the sandwich, center the batting on top of the wrong side of the backing fabric.

Center the quilt top, right-side up, on top of the batting and backing.

Follow the manufacturer's instructions to fuse the sandwich. If you choose not to use fusible batting, baste the sandwich using your preferred basting method.

Quilt the sandwich. To keep things simple, we quilted in the ditch. After all, the letters and motifs are large and will obscure a large part of the quilted area. Figure 4 shows how we quilted each one of the projects. Follow the order of the numbers and the directions of the arrows to quilt all the seams in the ditch.

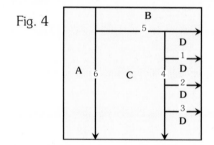

Fig. 4

Binding the quilt with the E pieces before you fuse the motifs ensures that none of the woolen pieces will lie under the binding. If you wish to bind after fusing, you can do so. Just keep the ¼" binding area clear of any of the letters or motifs.

LAYING OUT THE LETTERS AND MOTIFS

Review your project directions once more. Some of the projects include additional instructions regarding the fusing of the motifs.

Cut a piece of fusible web the same dimensions as the piece of wool to be used for the letters or motifs.

Trace the letters or motif onto the back of the fusible web. Leave about ¼" between letters. They are reversed; use them as is.

Following the manufacturer's directions, fuse the web to the back of the wool.

Cut letters and motif on the drawn lines. Remember not to use your best scissors. Wool LOVES to dull blades, so paper scissors are great for this.

Remove the backing paper from the letters and motifs.

Arrange the letters and motifs on the quilt top. To make your life easier and the project simpler, do this step directly on the ironing board.

Build multiple-piece motifs into one unit; use a pressing sheet.

Once you are satisfied with the placement of all letters and motifs, then and only then, fuse the wool to the quilt. Always remember to check the manufacturer's instructions for directions on how to best use the fusible material. Once you apply heat, the fuse is permanent!

THE FINAL TOUCH

You are almost done! Congratulations! All you need are a few finishing touches and you are on your way to giving someone a special, heartfelt "Thanks."

If you wish to embellish your quilt any further, now is your chance. Embellishment can make the quilt more personal, reflecting either the recipient's or your own personality. How much to embellish? That, our dear friend, is entirely up to you.

If you have not yet bound the quilt, do so now.

Sew two ½" plastic rings to the top back corners of the quilt. This is a small project and it does not require anything larger than that (like a sleeve) for support. Place the rings so that they "hide" behind the quilt when it is hung. If you prefer a sleeve, you can make one about ½" shorter than the width of the quilt and wide enough to fit the rod that will hold it. Hand-sew the sleeve to the top of the quilt back.

To complete the project, add a label to your quilt.

Don't forget this very important step! Identify yourself as the maker, as well as the date and your location. Add the name of the recipient, and if possible, pen a brief sentiment directed to the receiver—just a little something extra to remind them that you really, really appreciate them!

There are many ways to create a label. (Always remember to follow the manufacturer's directions when using these products):

♥ You can use a permanent fabric marker and write directly on the back of the quilt.

♥ You could use fabric that has been prepared for printing and print your message using a regular computer printer. Then just trim the printed fabric and fuse it to the back of the quilt using a piece of the same fusible material you used for the wool.

♥ You can also embroider the label and fuse it to the back of the quilt.

The point is to make a record of this small quilt so that, in time, its story is not lost and the reason behind the big thanks forgotten!

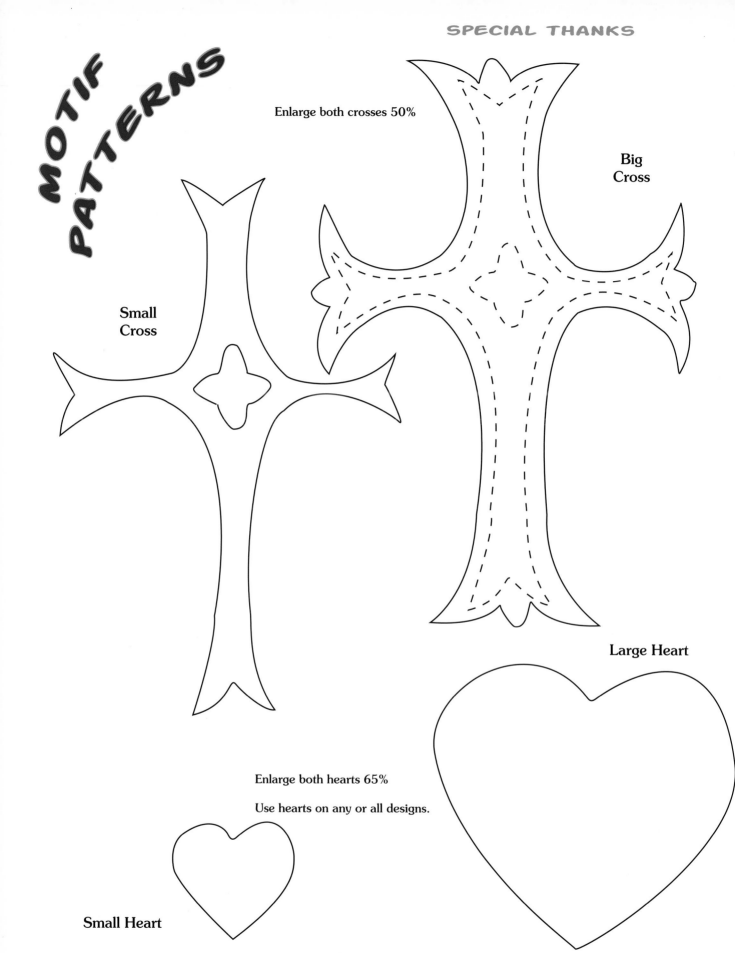

MOTIF PATTERNS

Enlarge both crosses 50%

Big Cross

Small Cross

Large Heart

Enlarge both hearts 65%

Use hearts on any or all designs.

Small Heart

MOTIF PATTERNS

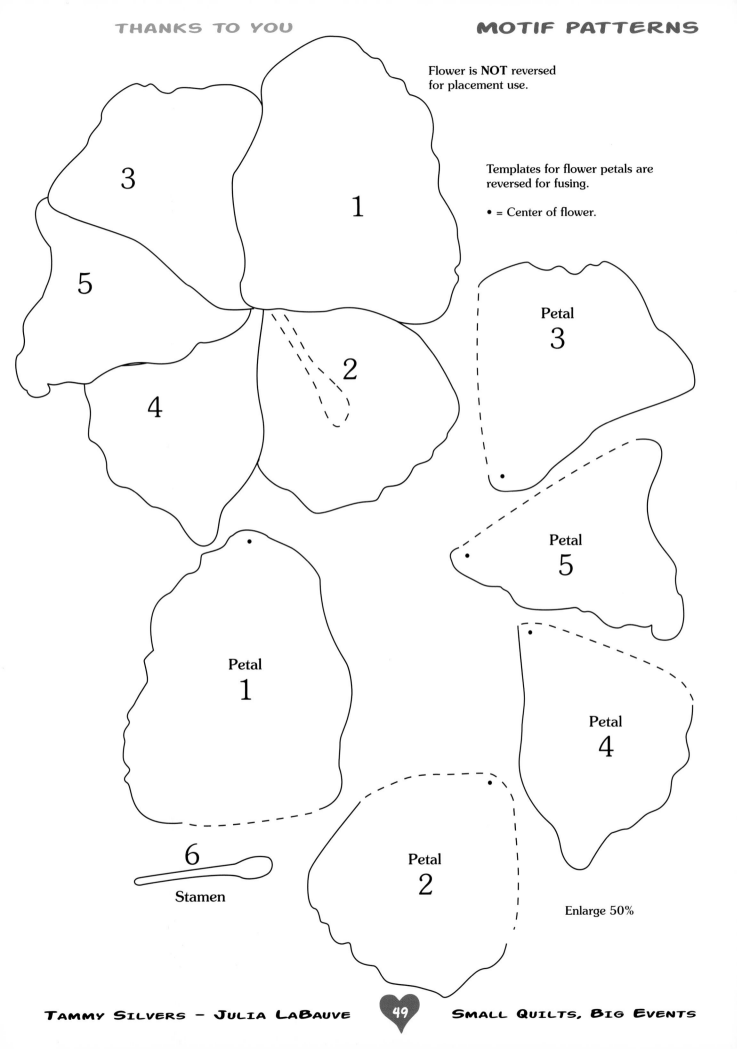

Flower is **NOT** reversed for placement use.

Templates for flower petals are reversed for fusing.

• = Center of flower.

3

1

5

2

4

Petal 3

Petal 5

Petal 4

Petal 1

Petal 2

6

Stamen

Enlarge 50%

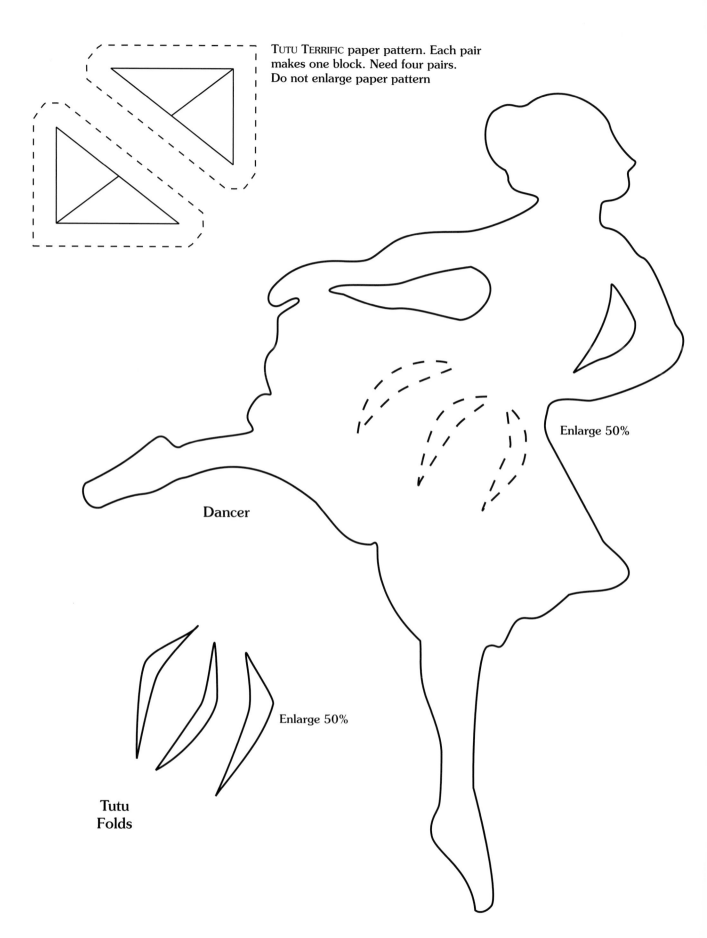

TUTU TERRIFIC paper pattern. Each pair makes one block. Need four pairs. Do not enlarge paper pattern

Enlarge 50%

Dancer

Enlarge 50%

Tutu
Folds

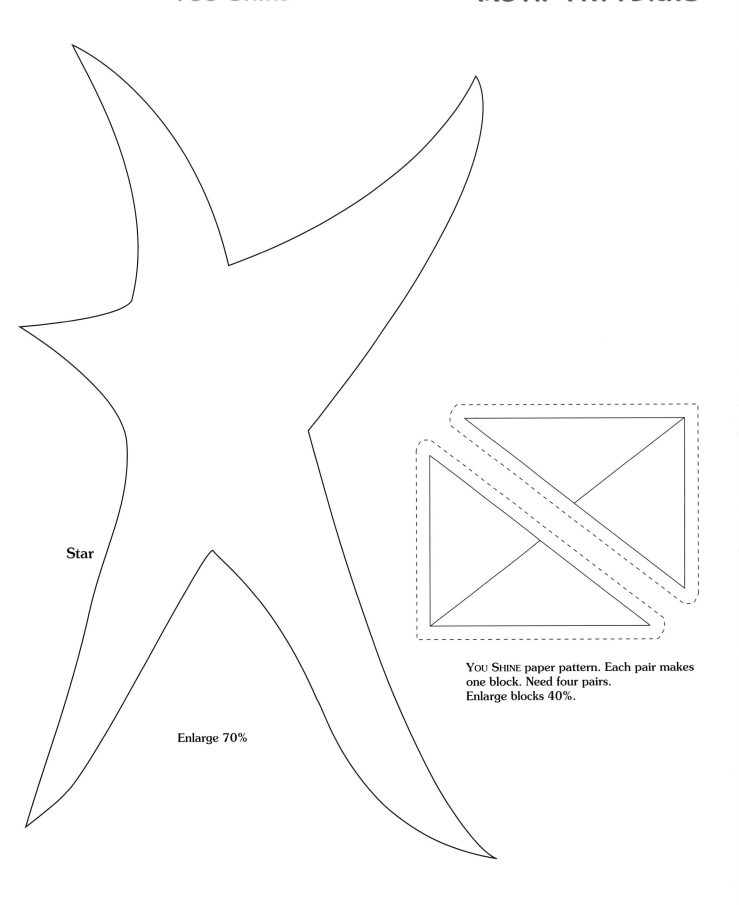

Star

Enlarge 70%

YOU SHINE paper pattern. Each pair makes
one block. Need four pairs.
Enlarge blocks 40%.

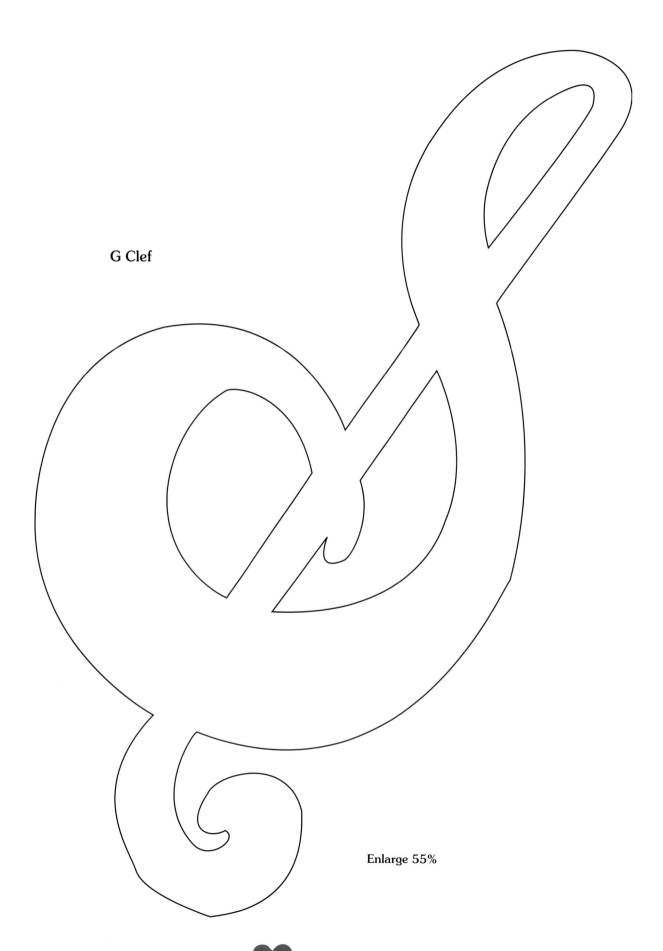

G Clef

Enlarge 55%

Sun

Spiral

Enlarge 70%

Big Heart

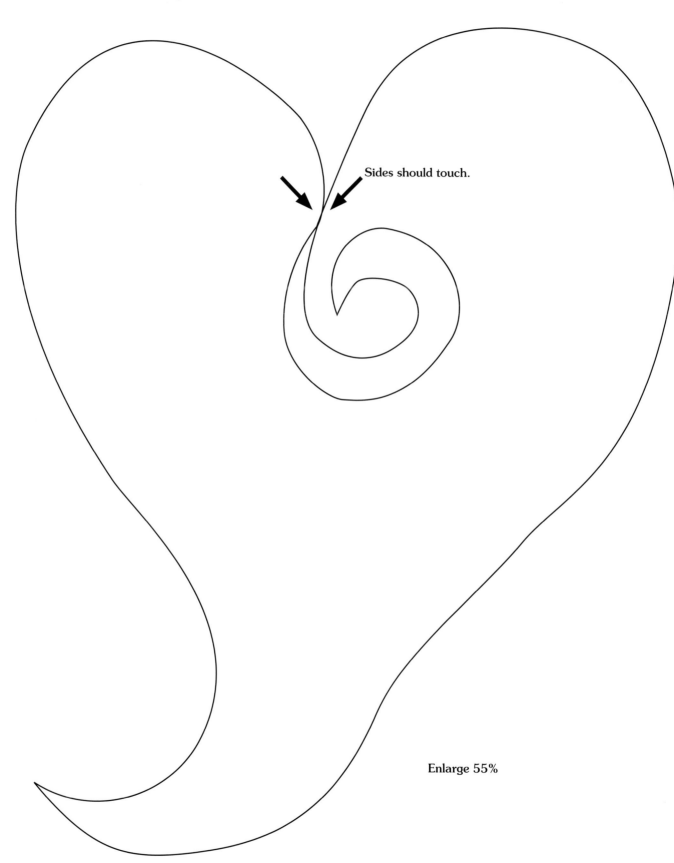

Sides should touch.

Enlarge 55%

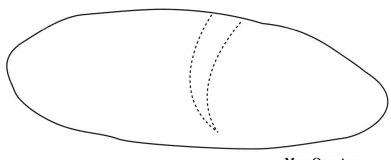

Mug Opening

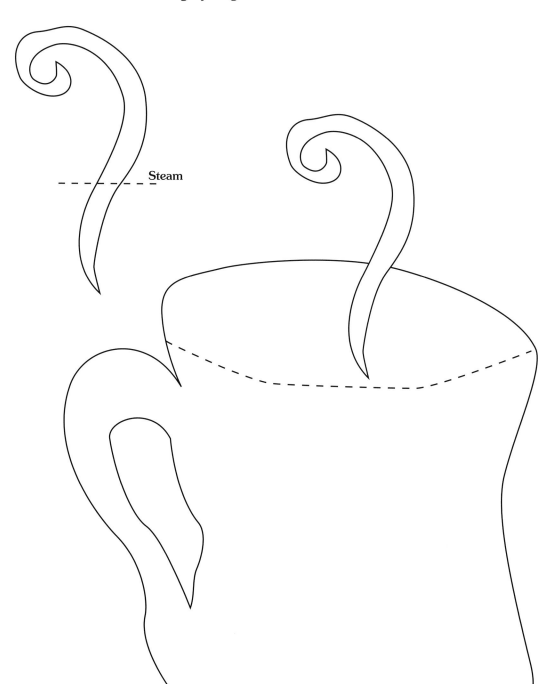

Steam

Enlarge 70%

Mug Body

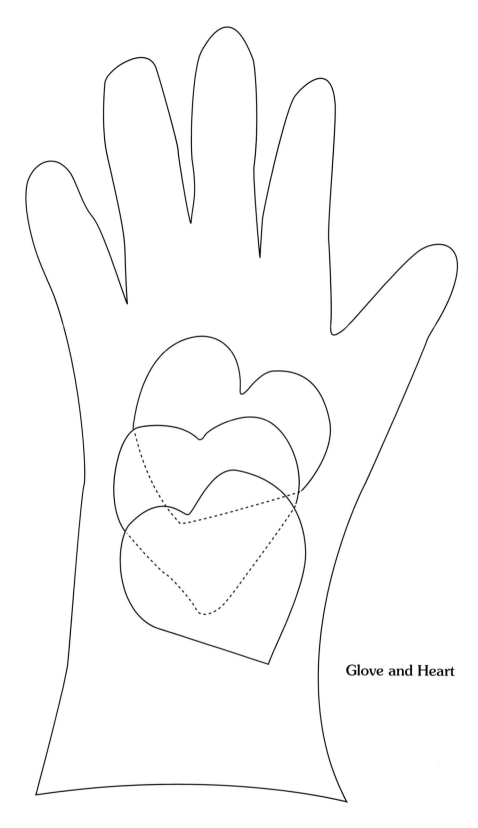

Enlarge 65%

Glove and Heart

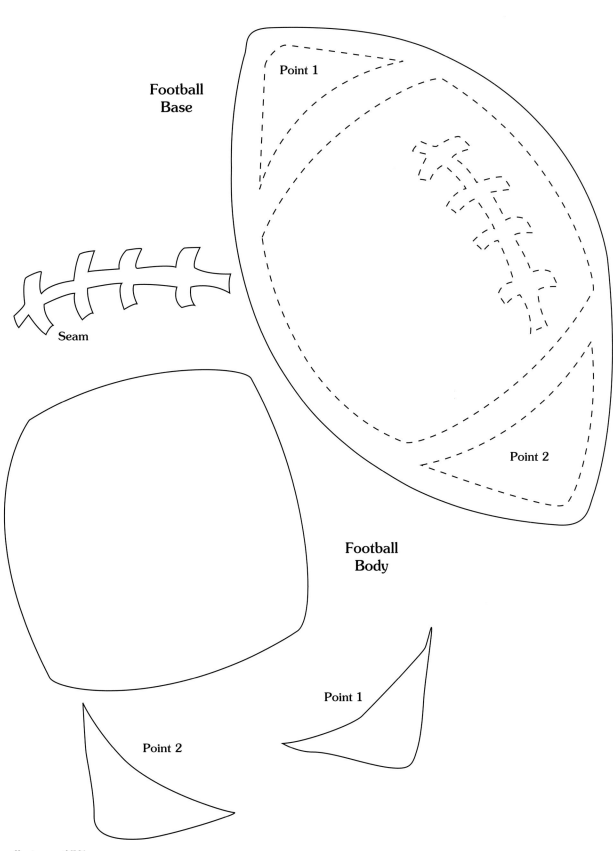

Football
Base

Point 1

Seam

Point 2

Football
Body

Point 1

Point 2

Enlarge all pieces 45%

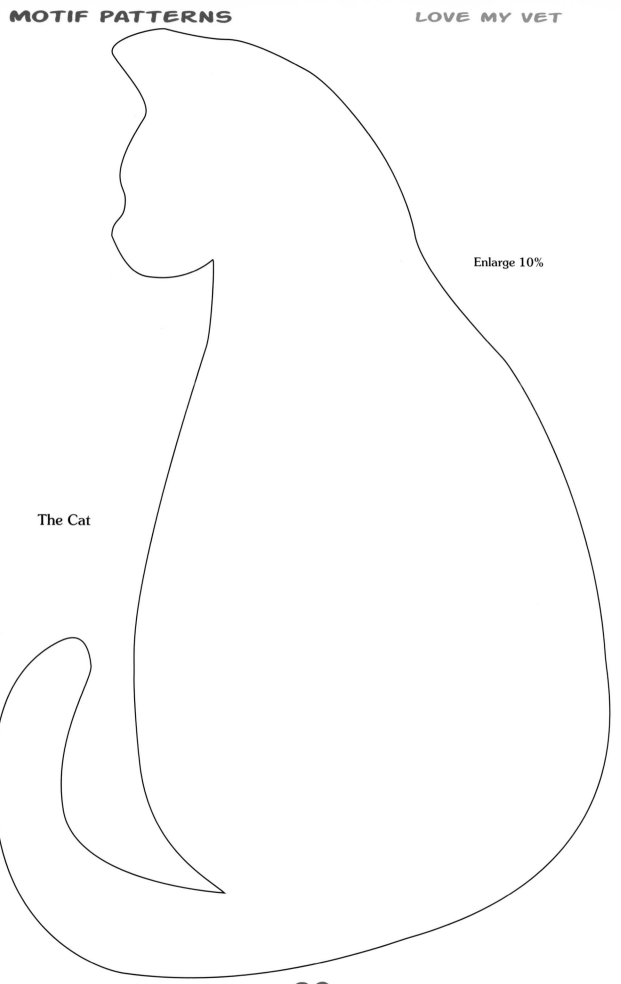

Enlarge 10%

The Cat

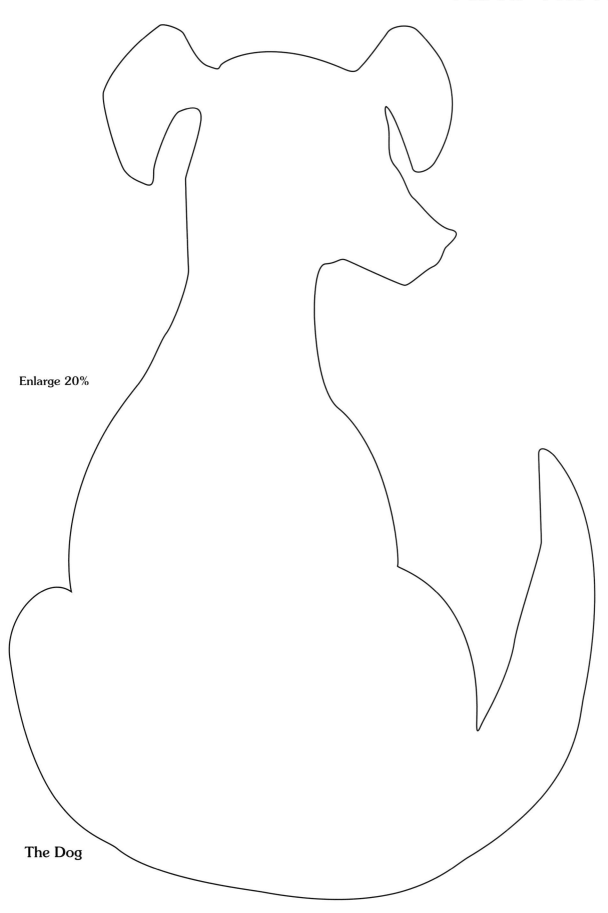

Enlarge 20%

The Dog

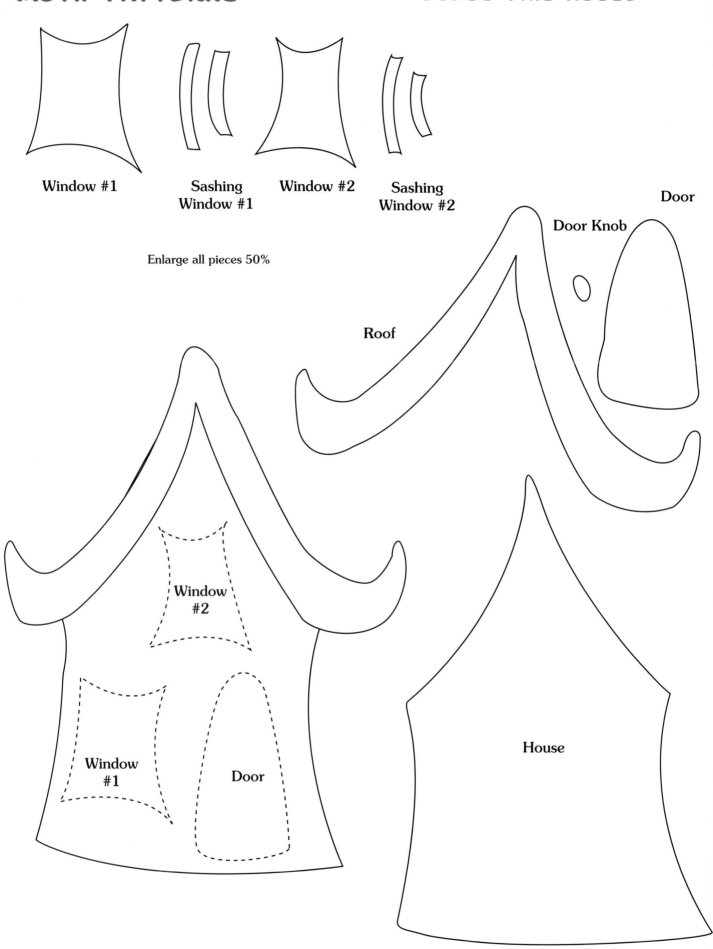

Window #1

Sashing Window #1

Window #2

Sashing Window #2

Enlarge all pieces 50%

Door

Door Knob

Roof

Window #2

Window #1

Door

House

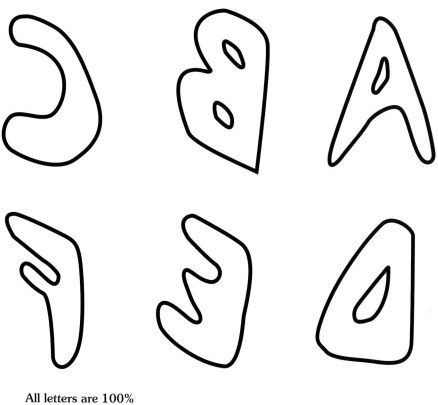

All letters are 100%

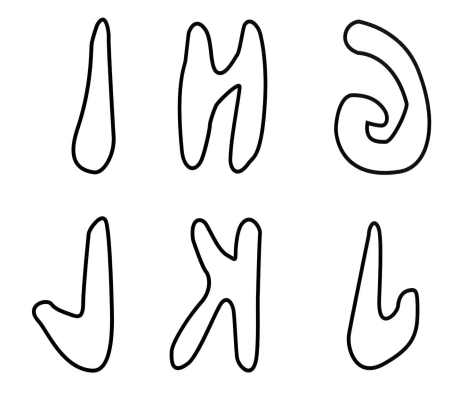

Turn M upside-down for W.

All letters are 100%

Wonder-Under® fusible web: www.pellonideas.com

Hobbs Heirloom Fusible Batting: www.hobbsbondedfibers.com

The Appliqué Sheet: www.bearthreaddesigns.com/

ABOUT THE AUTHORS

Tammy Silvers has been quilting since 1991. She has taught at a variety of fabric shops as well as local county Parks and Recreation facilities. She has also designed and self-published several of her own quilt patterns. Like any quilters enjoys working with most any fabric, however, she prefers batiks, bold prints, and chicken prints: "If it clucks, it goes in a quilt!" is her motto. Having a background in art and literature, Tammy looks for ways to use "words" in her work, be it in the fabric itself or by adding them to the piece. Tammy is a Georgia native and currently lives in Marietta with her husband, children, two dogs, and two cats.

Julia LaBauve began quilting in 1999, one of Tammy's many students. She prefers to work with fabrics that display bold motifs and intense colors such as batiks and ethnic fabrics, and also likes fabrics with lots of shine and metallic accents. With a background in science, Julia likes designs that are graphic and precise, both in the fabric and in the final piece. Originally from Puerto Rico, she now lives in Kennesaw, Georgia, with her husband and one dog.

In 2006 Tammy and Julia started Outside the Line Designs. As a team they have designed many quilts that play off of their combined interests and strengths, as well as their mutual love of vibrant fabric. Their designs are regularly published in a variety of quilt magazines.

Tammy and Julia count among their blessings being able to combine their long friendship with their love of quilting.

"It is always a good day when you can do what you love with those you love."

Julia LaBauve   Tammy Silvers

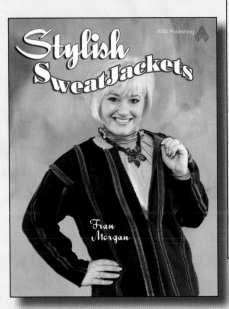

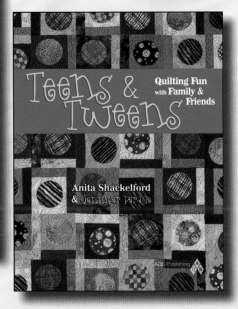

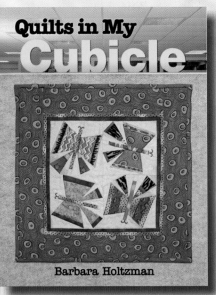